COPYRIGHT

Easy money.

Graeme Smith

PUBLISHED ON AMAZON.COM
BY
LABYRINTH BOOKS

DEDICATION:

This book is dedicated to my family.
Hele-ly (Ly).
        my wife:

Ingrid.
        our daughter:

Marie.
        my former wife:

Fiona, Natalie and Michael
        our children:

Georgie
        Michael's wife:

Pearl, Kiki and Martha.
        their children:

They have had to put up with me for many years and I thank them for that.
I hope this book gives them an idea into what occupied me much of the time.
They've all gained worthwhile and interesting careers without help from me.
I congratulate them for their achievements.

THANKS:

I greatly appreciate the contribution made to this book by comments and suggestions from:

Mike Barr – Adelaide, Australia

Richard Bruland - Los Angeles, USA

Tracey Creighton - Merimbula, Australia

Evelyn Dunphy – Maine, USA

Geoff Fellows – Wagga Wagga, Australia

Michelle Grace - Brisbane, Australia

Leanne Halls – North Sydney, Australia

Heidi Jeffries – Ferny Hills, Australia

Kathy Kay Voysey - Mudgee, Australia.

Vince Miller – 'Australian Artist' and 'International Artist'.

John Newell - Ontario, Canada

David Voigt – Yarramalong, Australia.

HOW TO USE THIS BOOK.

First think - then do.
Usually people don't think through things to the level they need to.
Because of that, they have projects instead of tasks on their "to do" list.
That leads to procrastination as it hasn't been broken down to a task level.

So go through your book once to understand it.
Go through it again.

Then start at the idea you would like to implement first.
Make notes of the steps you will need to take and the resources required.
Use these notes to create a step by step system for implementing the guide.
Often you will not refer back to an original, as you've created YOUR system.

The first question you ask and answer is "Why is this being done?"
How does this align with where you want to get to?
What are the strategic implications of doing this?
Does this fit with getting to a goal in the shortest and fastest amount of time?

What would it be like if it were totally successful?
Define it - what is success for this project and how will you know?

Now brainstorm all the tasks that are involved in your project.
It's important not to go linear too fast with this.
By linear, I mean step one, step two, step three, and step four.
You end up cutting off options.
Plan step one, two, and three, a specific step that might be number four.
If you start steps quickly, other ways of one, two or three may not appear.

The first third of any brainstorming session is really easy.
Just come up with lots of ideas.
The second third is challenging - go through ideas and see where they lead.
Then push yourself to think a little bit outside the box.
That's often where the big idea is!

That's where the most powerful way to get a project done fastest - is.
Most people never get to that level and end up short-changing themselves.
Then their project takes longer and they also procrastinate.
This final brainstorming part of the equation is incredibly important.

Once you fully brainstorm put your options into a linear sequence.
Then you can figure out what you've overlooked.
Everything becomes obvious as you get your tasks in order.
Now add missing steps and you have laid out your task list for this project.

Once you've organized the tasks into a linear process decide:
What things can you start immediately?
What can be started that is not dependent on things to occur before them?
Obviously that is step one.
Step five or six or twenty that don't really rely on anything else to get done.
You can get started on them right away too.

Now use a folder.
Write things you think of at the time and also cross off things as you do them.
Add in stuff that is relevant from time to time.

WHAT IS MARKETING?

Marketing is the process of finding buyers AND making sales
It is exactly the same process no matter what is being sold!
In some cases the process is simple like selling apples at a roadside stall.
It can be very complex like selling aero-planes for a government's air-force.
Most, including selling artworks, is somewhere in between these poles.

Think about fishing and you'll understand marketing.
Does a fisherman catch anything out in a desert?
NO, for there are simply no fish there.

You must market where there are possible buyers.
A fisherman must go where the fish are – where there is water.
That's a start but there are still no fish in a swimming pool are there?
They need to be in the right kind of water – a river, lake or at sea.

But different fish swim in different waters!
Sharks and marlin are in the ocean, while bream live mainly in rivers.
Likewise you must know who you are targeting with your marketing.
Will it be businesses, first home buyers, investors or what?
Each will need a different marketing program.

OK you are now in the right water for the kind of fish you are after!
Some species are nocturnal and they will not be caught during the day.
Your marketing needs to be when the target is likely to be most receptive.
Will it be at work, nights or weekends?

You are at the right place and time so how do you catch the fish?
Usually you'll have a fishing rod.
Is it the right kind for the fish you want to catch?
You won't catch a shark with the kind of rod that takes a trout!
Your marketing must be attractive to the people you are after.

Do you have the right bait?
Again different bait attracts different fish.
A carcass for the shark but just a worm for many other species.
Can you provide something that your target market will find attractive?

But throwing any bait into the water catches nothing at all!
The bait must be attached to a hook.
Without the fish taking the hook there is no catch.
Different hooks are needed for different kinds of fish.

Different hooks are also needed for different markets.
The right hook gets your market to take the next step to a purchase.
But this only needs to be a little step.

But hooks only catch the fish.
They're in the water, not your boat or beach, a hook is on the end of a line.
What is your line like, is it strong enough you the fish you are after?
Again this varies for the kind of fish.

How do you get your prospect to seriously consider what you sell?
For someone buying a print it will not need to be sophisticated.
But selling an original Renoir will be considerably more complicated.

That still no fish for the line has to have a reel for that to happen.
Again different reels for different fish.
The right reel allows you to bring the fish to the end of your fishing line.
But it's still not in the boat is it?

You must lift the fish out of the water into your boat or onto the beach.
Fishing nets do this so now you have your catch.
The fish is yours to do what you want with.

You can even sell the fish but who might want to buy?
It could be someone who sells fish for food or live for a fish-tank or pool.
They could even be for re-stocking natural water places.

Where can you find them?

You must look where the fish buyers are so follow the path of the fisherman.
And eventually you have a prospect asking can they buy.
You have made a sale AND you can make more sales the same way.

Making the sale is a five step process.

In order you work from the top through to the bottom group.

> **SUSPECTS** are people who possibly want what you have for sale.
> **PROSPECTS** are people likely to want what you have for sale.
> **BUYERS** are those who have bought what you are selling.
> **REPEAT BUYERS** continue to buy what you sell.
> **ADVOCATES** help you sell to others.

The reverse sequence is the order of importance to your sales.

INDEX: COPYRIGHT EASY MONEY.

Chapter One: A career opportunity.
1. Understanding and exploiting copyright laws.
2. Copying.
3. So what do you do?

1. Understanding and exploiting copyright laws.

Artists often want to know what constitutes a breach of copyright.
They use published photographs (from a magazine) as source material.
Maybe you paint on location, and also work from photos taken at other times.
You rarely find a perfectly composed photograph though.
So sometimes you use information from several photos.

Sometimes come across photos in old publications you want to use.
Getting written approval under the copyright law is difficult, if not impossible.
Sometimes a publishing firm no longer exists, changed its name or location.
Some images may have been around for twenty or more years.
In other cases no reply is received from the publisher.

Often there is no way you can find the copyright owner.
That's because the photograph has been detached from its source.

Like many artists, most of whom do not go to even this much trouble.
You go ahead and paint anyway.
Your need to generate paintings outweighs fear somebody may object.
If someone does emerge with a legitimate complaint, you have no problem.
You're OK for them to benefit financially from painting sale from copying.

Maybe you've read articles on copyright.
But did not find any reference to painting from published photographs.

Is yours is an interpretation rather than strictly a reproduction.
You feel comparing a painting with a photograph is like apples with oranges.
There are many differences in texture, colour and tone.

Even though the same basic structure (composition) is used.
An artist's identity is there by virtue of the style used in the painting.
So an impressionistic style may not be a reproduction of a photograph.

You wonder if a small part of a photo was used, would it be a copy.
What if information in the photograph is rearranged for a better composition?
How different does a result have to be before it doesn't infringe copyright?

You are probably breaching copyright.
There's no difference between copying a painting and copying a photograph.
You know the photographs are better than ones you take yourself.
That's why you use them.

Composition is linked directly to whoever took the original photograph.
Just as it is with painting.
I think you are aware of this.
That's why you attempted to contact the original photographer or publisher.
I prefer to take my own photographs, so I can get the compositions I like.

An interpretation is not usually an acceptable way out.
It depends on how much variation there is from the original.

As to the apples and oranges argument.
A copy is a copy whether done in the same medium or not (e.g. photocopy).
I guess that's it.
If it is recognizable as a copy.
It doesn't matter what medium, how well or badly done, or in what style.
It's a copy!

But the chance of a breach detected and prosecuted is quite small.
As long you take reasonable steps to contact the copyright holder,
The chance of prosecution is further reduced, by varying from the original.
Only you can decide whether this is a chance you are prepared to take.
What is your attitude to a situation like this?
Let's look at copying as a beginning to understanding copyright.

2. Copying.

There are two aspects of copying.
There's who does the copying (with or without permission).
And the owner of what is copied (who also owns the copyright).

Copying can be done legally and without permission, if it's for educational purposes.
Thus, copying is OK in an art class.
It's an excellent way of learning.
We learn by doing, in other words whilst painting.

Find out how Monet applied paint or arranged elements of a painting.
By painting a copy of one of his works.
This knowledge can then be applied to our own works.
So copying in these circumstances is fine.
It's one of the ways progress in our field is made.

In addition it's a way to liberate creativity.
For we can build on the efforts of those who have gone before.

A member of a group painting from the same motif is not copying.
The degree a teacher contributes to a result is of loss of originality.
In some classes many a student work is actually the teacher's!

A painter can become reliant on a teacher or another artist for ideas.
Then they may be missing something.
However this also applies if we depend on a limited range of our own ideas.
It is not where ideas originate but the range available and how they are used.
In fact whatever we do, we will miss something.

But what happens to the result?
This is the important question even when done legally as a way of learning.
A copy sold as your work it is dishonest and could be a breach of copyright.
If it's sold as the original artist's work that is also dishonest, it's a forgery.

What if you don't sell the work at all?

No problems but what happens after you die?

Will people then know this is yours or the artists, particularly if not signed?

This is how most forgeries come into existence.

They were done by a student but sold years later as an original work.

This explains why unsigned works are worth less than if authenticated.

Do you enter art competitions?

Usually copied works are banned or at the very least not anticipated.

If you enter an art competition, you are probably placing the work for sale.

If it's a copy, then you are being dishonest.

For you cannot any longer claim the work was just an educational exercise.

Equally if the work was done in a class, it may actually be the tutors.

At least your originality was compromised and you are basically dishonest.

Copying, unless a famous work, is very hard to detect, even by judges.

Even if it's entered in an art competition.

The same goes for work done in classes.

There will always be some dishonest people.

There are also many ignorant artists who just didn't know any better.

That's one of the problems with art competitions!

3. So what do you do?

You want to copy so you can learn things.
But you'd like to avoid any repercussions for having done so?
The best idea is to copy the artist's signature so it clearly isn't your work.
AND also put in your own signature so it clearly isn't the original artist's work.

Then, even centuries later people will know the work is a copy by you.
Attach information on the back of the work but that gets lost over the years.

An artist may copy someone else's artwork and make it their own.
They aren't allowed to sell them without permission of the original artist.
They feel if their copy is changed sufficiently then it will no longer be a copy.
But it must be changed sufficiently it's not recognized as the original work.

If you paint animals copying photographs is obviously very tempting.
People with telephoto lenses can take shots no artist would get to even see.
There's nothing wrong with taking your own photos though.
But that's a bit hard of you want to paint a polar bear isn't it?
You need to make enough changes to be unrecognizable as the photo.
But still a polar bear (or whatever).

Is there's a middle point when it's impossible to define if's a copy?
Otherwise you need to get permission from the copyright owner.
In most animal cases the publisher or the photographer.
That's a hassle but that's the law.

My suggestion is practice polar bears (or whatever) first.
Copy from photos taken from the sources that you seek to use.
Destroy the copies, so don't use best quality canvas etc.

You can't destroy what you have learned.
Do enough polar bears that way and you can paint them from memory.
Then copyright will no longer be a concern as they are your bears.

But once you understand the opportunities the copyright laws provide.

You'll realize you can earn more money for very little extra work!

AND

You won't need to copy anything at all!

Also use copyright as a bargaining chip to leverage opportunities.

It may take a couple of years before everything is in place.

That's no reason to wait until Christmas, next year, or when the 'right' time is.

All that means is the whole process is delayed.

But there needs to be work done before there is any return.

There's little actual expense initially, a start can be made if time is available.

Other projects dealt with (foregone, delayed, accelerated) for a speedy start.

But maybe not!

Chapter Two: Copyright.

1. Let's look at copyright?
2. Who owns copyright?

1. Let's look at copyright?

Sometimes there is a circle with the letter 'c' and the copyright owner.
This tells people the work is protected by copyright.
But a work is protected even without this symbol.

Most artists these days know a little about copyright.
If you venture into the world of reproductions, you are likely to know more.
It's basically about permission to copy an original artwork (the right to copy).
But just to make sure you really do understand here is the essence.

Copyright is a law about the right to copy for commercial purposes.
A detailed and legally correct interpretation of these laws is available.
Contact the Arts Law Centre of Australia (www.artslaw.com.au) in Sydney.
Legal organizations in countries with copyright laws have similar publications.
The laws are quite simple and straightforward.
They don't vary much from one country to another, except if they don't exist!
I can't see why anyone would be confused.

Copyright is about the form of a creation.
This might a work, manuscript, poem, or score.
It does not concern the ideas within the copy!
A copier has their own ideas (make a copy) even if an exact copy is made.
The idea cannot be copied.

The difference from the original determines if there is a copy or not.
Merely changing a few elements will probably not be sufficient.
Claims of no longer a copy of an original but a new work won't be enough.
The originator can equally claim the opposite.

It is NOT permissible to reproduce a work just by making changes.
An example would be just altering the colours.
If it's possible to compare work and copy, and important parts are identified.
Then permission to copy is necessary.
This even applies to scanning an image to a computer.
Then altering it to make a new work, by someone other than you.
A copyright owner's permission is needed to copy an image, and also alter it.

A judge or a jury will decide who is right.
You will have to be prepared to make your case at that level.
Moving things, leaving something out, putting something in isn't enough.

Even with no intention to publish a copy permission may be needed.
Copyright is about copying for commercial purposes.
It's not necessarily carried out by the copier.
It's OK for art galleries or museums to copy a work for archival purposes.

There may be more than one copyright to some works.
A photograph of a paintings has copyright to the painting and the photo too.

How long does copyright last?
As a general rule, copyright lasts for the life of the creator plus fifty years.
Copyright expires on your works 50 years after you die.
This will apply no matter who owns the copyright at that time.
Duration is measured by the creator's life, even if they didn't own copyright.
Once copyright has expired it cannot be revived.

2. Who owns copyright?

A creator (artist, author, playwright, poet) owns the work and copyright.
These are separate and can be sold, given away or retained independently.
Copyright is permission to reproduce or copy the work.

Copyright is just like any other property you own at the time of death.
When you die the copyright will pass to someone else usually your family.
But you could decide differently and it may be transmitted by will.
If there's no will then according to the various laws that apply in that situation.
If copyright has not specifically been bequeathed, it passes to the next of kin.

With very few exceptions copyright in only owned by you.
There has to be written signed document to assign copyright, or part thereof.
It says someone else owns copyright or some portion of it.
Thus it follows you may assign copyright to someone else.

Unless clear evidence of copyright ownership passing to another party.
Then the creator or their heirs still own it.
The sale of a painting or other artwork does **NOT** automatically sell copyright.
It is a separate saleable aspect so you can sell copyright and retain the work.
Or even sell the work to someone else entirely!

An exception is if you are on staff and create a work as employment.
Then the employer is the owner of copyright to that work.
Perhaps you are paid as photographer for the local newspaper.
Copyright on photographs taken by you in your work is owned by the paper.

Paparazzi are photographers who own copyright on their photographs.
They are not employees.
If you work freelance then you own the copyright.
A work is a photograph, portrait or engraving created in return for payment.
In this case, the client is usually the first owner of copyright.
This is basically a commissioned arrangement.
However this does not apply for say paintings.

Another exception is if the work was created for a government.
The government is usually the first owner of copyright, even if it is a painting.
Well you'd expect something like that from government wouldn't you?

These situations can be changed by agreement between the parties.
In addition, a commissioning client, is not the owner of copyright.
But usually is entitled to use the work for the reasons it was commissioned.
They will need the copyright owner's permission for any other purpose.
That includes authorizing use of the work by others.
A publisher commissions you a series of paintings for place mats.
Cannot just publish prints as well, without your added permission.
Giving the added permission may mean new terms are negotiated.

When selling copyright you can ask for attribution.
You should be recognized as the creator of the original work.
Even if you do not ask, there is an obligation on the copyright owner to do so.

You can ask that any copies be faithful reproductions, or not.
Publishers of digitized material often publish art works at low resolution.
This allows viewing on a screen but doesn't produce a good printed copy.
You could insist on this as a way of discouraging unauthorized reproductions.

You may not want your work to be published other than full resolution.
It's up to you, but the copyright holder must know what the situation is.
You could insist information about copyright is published in a digitized image.

It's a good idea for permission to be in writing.
There's documentation showing what exactly is covered by an agreement.
There is also less likely to be a dispute about what was covered.

Is your country is a party to various international copyright treaties?
You're protected in those countries which are also parties to the agreements.
Check your own country to see if there are differences to those I've outlined.

Permission, which is short of complete copyright is called license.
Permission is even needed to reproduce just a part of one of your works.
If the part is important in relation to the whole work.

From all this it follows that the owner of a work may not own copyright.
In fact that's how it is in many cases.
But the owner of the work can sell, exhibit or donate that work.
NOT the copyright owner.

Chapter Three: Prints and copyright.

1. But before we get to that what is a print?
2. What's the link between copyright and prints?
3. Sell copyright to a publisher.

1. But before we get to that what is a print?

Do we know what we are talking about, what is a print and printing?
Printing makes multiple images each being identical to others in the series.
Each image is called a print and a series of prints is referred to as an edition.
For an image to be a print, there is more than one identical print produced.
Common prints are pictures in books, placemats, greeting cards, posters.

In the art world 'print' refers to two different kinds of printing process.
They're 'original' prints or 'reproduction' prints, but often they're called prints.
Usually this doesn't matter, sometimes it does, so how are they different?

What are reproduction prints?
If there's an image, from which prints have been copied, it's a reproduction.
It is a reproduction of an original work.

The original has been executed in a different medium from the print.
An oil painting is reproduced as an offset lithographic print ('Mona Lisa').
Sometimes a print from a watercolour can even look much like the original.
But it's still not the same as the original, it's **NOT** a watercolour.

An original print is not a copy of anything.
It's the original, there are others the same, that is a characteristic of any print.
It's like identical twins or triplets, they all look the same.

But there's no original from which each has been copied.
Original prints are from a plate, screen, stone, photocopier or computer.

For a reproduction print to exist there is a way to copy the original.
Photography is common but it is scanned on a computer or photocopied.
There'll be various other electronic copying devices invented in the future.
A century or more ago if an original work was copied, it was an engraving.

But an original print is always done in the medium of the print.
Screen-printing, etching, lithography or other print process has been used.
These prints were done by the artist or in collaboration with another artist.
The second artist may do the actual printing.
They're called 'artist prints' but most importantly, it is not a copy of anything.

To repeat, to be a print, there has to be more than one image produced.
Each of these images should be the same as the others.

This creates confusion between reproduction and original prints.
But keep in mind in one case they are multiple copies of an artwork.
Whereas in the other they are clones (like twins) and not copies of anything.

What are the advantages of prints?
More than one copy is available in each print edition.
They're more obtainable than paintings which are only one-off works.
The commercial law of supply and demand means they're more affordable.
A designer dress costs more than an off the rack similar piece of clothing.
A hand-built car (prototype) costs much more than a production model.
An architect designed house costs more than a project home and so on.
It's not just the cost of production that makes one-off items more expensive.
The greater or lesser supply of those goods affects their price too.

Reproduction prints make available an image that was not otherwise.
For example the 'Mona Lisa'.

Original prints bring into existence something that didn't previously.
Some artists have produced both original prints and reproductions prints.
It's possible to see an economic relationship between the two print species.

An original print will be much higher in price than the reproduction.
But much lower than for a one-off artwork.

2. What's the link between copyright and prints?

Copyright is the right to copy an original creative work.
This is not limited to art work, it also applies to literature and musical scores.
With literature selling copyright is the main way authors make money.
Publishers pay for the right to copy the author's story in a book form.
The author keeps the manuscript, or original work.
It has some value, but not as much as the copyright.

Just as with authors, copyright exists in relation to any artwork.
Authors own copyright and manuscript, an artist owns artwork and copyright.
They may be sold together or separately.

Many artists don't realize this, thinking they sell both together.
Selling the artwork does **NOT** automatically sell the copyright.
Most buyers do not realize this either, although publishers do.
The most common way for copyright to be sold by an artist is to a publisher.
The publisher produces prints of the work, in a book, magazine or as cards.

An artist usually owns copyright unless specifically transferred.
Ownership of copyright gives an owner a legal right to copy an original work.
It's the right to copy that's owned not necessarily the work itself.

Someone buys a painting but that doesn't mean they can print cards.
Not even featuring this image, to send to their friends at Christmas.
Perhaps you aren't worried about this, but you own the copyright anyway.
It's legal to produce cards of your painting owned by someone else.

When selling copyright, it can be transferred in a limited way.
You can sell copyright to an image for a certain reproduction process.
But not any other kind.
This means a publisher has copyright to produce place mats from a painting.
If they want to produce cards then they must negotiate again.
Or you can sell that form of copyright to someone else.

Limitations can also apply in other ways too.

A common limitation is the number to be produced (say 500).

A publisher produces prints but if they want more they must renegotiate.

Geographical limits can also apply.

The prints can only be sold in Australia, London, or where you care to name.

World rights are still to be negotiated.

3. Sell copyright to a publisher.

Selling copyright can be a very attractive proposition.
An artist keeps the painting, which is worth more, and receive income too.
Successful reproduction print artists of the art business, are well rewarded.
You'd be surprised at how well some print artists live, but it is competitive.

What advantages are there?
Let's say you've made it into print.
Advantages flow from selling copyright this way apart from money earned.
Not the least is considerable promotion by wide availability of your images.
Just think about how well known Darcy Doyle is as an artist in Australia?
Other countries have equivalents known by their prints (Norman Rockwell).
You can benefit by sales of all your original works too, not just those in prints.

There are other advantages in selling copyright to a publisher.
You don't have the cost of producing the prints, books, cards or magazines.
Also you don't have the cost of selling these items.

Both of costs are quite considerable and even impossible for an artist.
Artists who produce their own prints or cards know how expensive this is.
Particularly the cost of selling.
There's a good chance they don't have the know-how to do these things too.
Again particularly selling to the mass market.
Negotiating with printers, paper wholesalers and photographers takes time.
Experience is needed to produce the best result.

But these difficulties are small compared to setting up a sales network.
You must penetrate a large marketplace to avoid drawers of unsold prints.
It's usually a good idea, to leave these things to the publisher too!

Not all artworks are equally suited to this type of promotion.
Prints are sold in large numbers to cover costs of publishing and distribution.
They should also make the publisher and yourself a profit.
Publishers' sales efforts are thus aimed at the mass market.

So to be successful, a print must appeal to many people.
Most people do not have an artistic background.
Successful prints rely for their appeal on non-artistic factors.
By this I mean no art knowledge is required of the observer.

The subject featured is very important.
Images based on reality, or decorative requirements, have best chance.
Images evoking feelings of nostalgia or familiarity, are strong print sellers too.
Basically most prints are bought for their subject matter or colour.
For artists whose work is in this category, original prints are a way to go.
Appealing to few art connoisseurs is not a proposition.

Talk to a picture framer about what prints sell and you'll get the idea.
If your work is of this sort, it is likely to be suited to reproduction as prints.
Then give publishers a call and see if you can sell copyright to some images.
But, even with the right image, there are dangers too.

How do you negotiate with publishers?
The publisher is more used to bargaining with artists than you.
They often get copyright and the painting for the cost of the painting.
This is particularly if you're really just keen to sell the painting.
But remember you are selling two separate entities.
You may sell one or the other, or both.
But make sure you are happy with the price you obtain in each case.

The publisher wants the copyright more than the painting.
So this is your main point of discussion.
Negotiate an attractive fee for copyright and add the painting free if want.
The painting is really a bargaining chip in these discussions.

How much is copyright worth anyway?
First of all find out what the average sales percentages are.
Do they sell 10%, 50%, 95% or what?

What sort of price do the prints normally sell at?
How much of this goes to the retailer, the publisher and the artist?
Ask the publisher what sort of print run they're considering with this image.

Then do your sums.
A publisher sells 50% of a print run and plans to print 2000 to sell at $25 ea.
You can work out the likely return if the royalty is, say 10%.
In this case it would be $2500.
Thus an outright sale of copyright for this amount might be reasonable.
Authors also receive 10% of sales as their usual royalty payment.

Keep in mind that a first time print artist may not be able to sell 50%.
It was an average so there's an argument for accepting a lower start figure.
But ask for more with each additional print, and print run.

You can sell copyright outright for an agreed sum or as sales royalty.
Usually the latter is the most rewarding, but the risk is greater.
You do **NOT** have any control over the sales process.
AND you have **NO** real way of knowing what those sales might be (at first).
You must trust the publisher to pay promptly and correctly, for sales made.
You don't usually have access to the publisher's books.
So there is a potential problem and artists have been taken advantage of.
However if you cannot trust the publisher, you should not deal with them.

Outright sale eliminates the trust problem.
But for the publisher it requires money up front.
They're less likely to do this unless the amount you want is very attractive.
You could try to obtain a royalty on prints produced rather than those sold.
But this'll be hard to achieve.

As mentioned earlier, copyright may be transferred in a limited way.
You may limit production to a specific number of copies.
That could be one, five hundred, five thousand, a million or whatever.
After that the publisher must renegotiate for any additional print run.

There may also be geographic limitations related to sales of the copies.
They're sold locally, your state, Australia, USA, the world, or where you like.
There may be other limits the owner (you) and a potential owner agree to.
One is a sunset clause, so after a certain time copyright reverts to you.

Having your work published is real business.
There's tough negotiating with an experienced negotiator.
Pick your way through pitfalls and possibilities and you can get a good deal.
So do be careful, for it's possible to fall into a hole.
It's a good idea to ask the publisher for name, address and phone numbers.
Of other artists published by that firm.
Don't just take those supplied for they are likely to be the most successful.
Ask for others by looking through the print range and select some at random.

Contact these artists and ask them anything you want to know.
Take care if a publisher can't supply names, address, and phone numbers.
Perhaps most of the prints are from overseas sources.
But it may be an indicator of a poor relationship with the artists.
Negotiating with publishers may not be easy.
But if you are successful in selling copyright, it can be very rewarding.

Chapter Four: Making money.

1. Can you make money from copyright?
2. Who are likely buyers of copyright?
3. Can you value copyright properly?
4. Do your sums and sell copyright!

1. Can you make money from copyright?

Most artists these days know something about copyright.
It's basically about permission to copy an original artwork (the right to copy).
You own copyright of works done by you, unless specifically transferred.
A sale of an artwork does not automatically mean the copyright was sold.

It is a separate saleable aspect.
So you can sell the copyright of a work and retain the work itself.
Or even sell the work to someone else entirely!

Copyright is worth money separately from any for the original work.
The most common situation is when an artist sells copyright to a publisher.
The publisher copies on plates, calendars, prints, greeting cards place mats.

But let's look at selling copyright from a different perspective?
Think about all the artworks ever produced.
It's a huge number even if we don't know how many exactly.
Of this number how many do you think actually earn money for copyright?
Not too many in comparison to the number painted, is it?

Vast numbers of artworks and artists receive NO money for copyright.
That's because they believe there's only one way to get money for copyright.
That's by selling to a publisher.

Well it doesn't have to be like this.
There is another way, which you will not have heard about before, anywhere.
Yes this is a sellable component of their art activity.

Earn money from copyright without getting into publishing at all!
Each time you sell artworks have the copyright for sale, for a small premium.
Perhaps 10% is a reasonable premium for copyright, but it's up to you.

That's what authors get when they sell copyright.
A person buys your painting for $1000 and for $100 extra receives copyright.
It could be the $1100 painting includes $100 for copyright.

Notice you will receive 10% extra income for NO extra work.
Well, not quite, for not all people will want the copyright, but many will.
Whatever the number, it's still extra money for no additional artistic work.
It is money you would not otherwise have obtained.
But your client pays extra and receives something quite valuable to them.

There are other advantages too.
Let's say someone wants to buy your work, but at a discount.
In this day and age it's happening more and more often.
Well then, you say 'OK I'll sell it to you, but without the copyright.'

You now have an extra bargaining chip.
It's something extra you can take off.
So a sale at the full price for a painting (without the copyright) is increased.

Some artists worry about people now owning the copyright will do.
There's not much bad they can do, unless you have sold a terrible painting.
That sort of painting should be destroyed rather than sold anyway.
But here are some possible scenarios:

Most buyers would do absolutely nothing.
However ownership of copyright adds value to the painting.
That's because the new owner may sell it on at a later date.
Promote ownership of copyright in this way as an add-on bonus.
Owners like to know they can reproduce a work, even if they never do.

What if a buyer did do something?
Perhaps a set of cards printed?
This promotes you and has not cost anything whatsoever.

If in an upper-income bracket your image goes to similar people.
This is just about the best word of mouth advertising money simply can't buy!

It can only do you some good.
Unless you believe certain kinds of promotion are good and others are not.
If this is your way, then you may not be interested in selling copyright at all.
But you forgo income if you take this path but now at least you have a choice

You can sell copyright in a limited way too.
Thus you can prevent what you consider to be undesirable promotions.
But still obtaining money from your asset.
Say the copyright holder can't use the image on a poster without permission.
Limitations may be for a specific number of copies (1, 100, whatever).
There are geographic limitations to copy sales (no local, in USA, the world).
There may be other limitations that you and the potential owner agree on.

Limitations reduce attractiveness for the buyer.
The copyright holder must be able to reproduce your work in some way.
Otherwise they haven't really obtained copyright.
A new owner has copyright to produce greeting cards for personal use only.
And they are not to be sold.

It's up to you to construct the deal.
There must be something for the buyer or no sale (of copyright) takes place.

What if there's a painting you'd like to make a print of yourself?
Just don't sell the copyright with this one or reserve that aspect to yourself.

Selling copyright is a powerful added value factor to bring extra sales.
As well as extra income from each sale it costs you nothing extra to do.

2. Who are likely buyers of copyright?

Yes, it's someone who wants to make copies.
That's usually also the person who wants to own the original work!
Sell buyers copyright was suggested first in 'Art Professional' 016.
It's an idea that, to my knowledge, has never previously been suggested.
So few artists have considered making extra money this way.

Here's what you do.
When you sell an artwork, also have copyright for sale, for a small premium.
Perhaps 10% is a reasonable amount for copyright, but this is up to you.
A person can buy a $1000 painting and for an extra $100 have copyright too.
Or it could be the $1100 painting includes the copyright.

What about value adding too?
Selling copyright can be a powerful added value factor to bring extra sales.
As well as extra income from each sale it really costs nothing to try.

Just in case you are not sure what I'm getting at.
You (or your gallery) advertises your works at whatever their normal price.
Then for NO extra, or only 10% (as you choose) they also obtain copyright.
Print your own cards without any hassle (etc.).

Thus promoting buying a work doesn't automatically mean copyright.
But it doesn't stop there either!

Are there other copyright buyers?
There's another large group of people who are potential buyers of copyright.
Sell copyright to people who have ALREADY bought your work!
Yes, sell to people who own your paintings now.

Contact all people who have bought your work in the past.
Offer them the copyright, either outright or a limited version, as you choose.
Sell the copyright for; say 10% of the work's value.

This won't be easy.
You won't know all your past buyers, or their present whereabouts.
Also not all will want to buy copyright, for they love and have the painting.

An intention to sell copyright is a way to negotiate with a gallery.
Get from them and others who sold works in the past names and addresses.
They can sell copyright for you and open up possible sales of your work.

You might have to split the copyright income in this situation.
You discover 30% of past buyers and 25% of these want to buy copyright.
Let's say you sold at $500 average and you've sold 900 works to 850 clients.

What could this mean to you?
It means you've found 255 people who've bought $13,500 worth of paintings.
Of these 64 buy copyright on $3375 worth of paintings.
Copyright sales at say 10% of value will thus bring in $337.50.

The figures are mythical, but I think you'll get the idea.
$337.50 costs perhaps $47.25 postage, +a little for envelopes and paper.
Maybe there was a similar amount in phone calls?
Whatever it's a cheap way of earning money – actually money for nothing!

You may say but that's not really much money.
Even so you may as well have it as not.
More importantly you've opened up lines for further sales of your work.
That could make the whole exercise very worthwhile.

Could it be even better?
The most likely interested buyers of copyright are also likely to be known.
The buyers of more expensive works and multiple buyers are easier to track.
Than once only buyers of less expensive works.

Take these facts into account and figures are likely to be much better.
I used averages, real figures are likely to be at the upper end of the scale.

Copyright marketing gives a chance to contact again those clients.
This could lead to new purchases of similar valued works.

What about the steak knives?
Not only is this a way you can capitalize on sales already made.

But you can do it at to-day's values!
For example a work sold in 1980 for $500 is now worth $2000.
Because you are selling copyright this year, you'll sell it at present values.
Apply this thinking to the previously mentioned figures.
The possibility of selling copyright to past buyers looks very attractive indeed.

You also realize this is a way to capitalize on rising price for your work.
Now you catch up with those early buyers, who bought cheaply.
To obtain copyright they must pay at the present enhanced value of works.

With no copyright sales this reinforces rising value of your work.
It does so in a very real way for the buyer.
They can understand how their purchase has appreciated.
They buy into a rising trend by adding copyright to investment in your career.
As before most copyright buyers will do absolutely nothing with it.

But they're getting added value from their original purchase.
Again those that do something promote you at no cost to yourself.
If there's a particular painting you really want to make a print of yourself.
Don't sell the copyright with that work, or sell copyright but in a limited way.
For example the painting owner has copyright to produce greeting cards.
But they are for his/her use only and are not to be sold commercially.

The more you think along these lines, the more attractive the idea is.
It's still a little difficult if you can't sell your paintings in the first place though.
But that's another matter entirely.

3. Can you value copyright properly?

How can you get the right price in a copyright sale?
Let's say you have a painting that is to be used on a wine label.

In this situation you are looking at two separate sales.
Charge your usual rate, or more (it's the 'wine label painting') for the work.
What you charge for copyright is for you to negotiate.
Whilst you may consider expenses as a basis for this you do not have to.
Also whilst the price of the painting could also be a basis, it need not be.

Basically the main consideration of value will be:
The vineyard's desire to own and use the image on their label.
And your desire to also see it used this way.

How do you price copyright?
It may seem hard to put a price on this, but it's the same as pricing a work,
Except in that case you have past sales as a basis for calculations.
Authors usually receives 10% of all sales of works published for copyright.
As you are no doubt aware this can be quite substantial.

Thus you can negotiate a sum of money for copyright.
This is by far the most common way.
But you can negotiate for a % of sales, as many reproduction print artists do.
In the case of a wine label, the negotiation could be along these lines.

Say the cost of the label represents 10% of the cost of a bottle of wine.
You could ask for 10% of this, or 1% of each bottle of wine with your label.
Initially this may not be much, but depending on sales it could add up.
Payments could be made monthly.

Let's say this line of thinking attracts you.
Find out about how many bottles (cases = 12 bottles) sold last year.
How many do they expect to sell with your label on?
Do these calculations outweigh the sum of money you feel you could get?

Then that's the way to go, unless you need money now.
The calculations give you a guide as to how much to ask as a sum of money.
This is probably something less than residual payments would earn.

But there are the steak knives too?
Also negotiate for prints of the painting when the labels are printed.
Possibly even paid for by the winery.
These could be sold at the cellar door, and/or through your usual outlets.
Don't get too many done though.
It is better to be sold out, than forever selling the same print.
Take this approach and you leverage the artwork sale more than before.
Negotiating the sale of prints is a **THIRD** sale for you from the same painting.

As indicated elsewhere most copyright buyers do absolutely nothing.
But they **ARE** getting extra value from their original purchase.
Copyright owners who do something promote you at no cost to yourself.

If there's a particular painting that you'd like to make a print of yourself.
Then don't sell copyright on that one, or sell it in a limited way.
A copyright owner can produce greeting cards for his/her use only.

Think of copyright on these lines and the more attractive the idea is.
Of course it's still difficult if you can't sell your paintings in the first place.
But that's a different problem.

4. Do your sums and sell copyright!

I learned a great deal about how a professional artist can make money.
A lot of it since closing my gallery in 1997.
This probably sounds unbelievable to many people yet it is the case.
I think it is mainly because I have focused myself on that topic.
So I am always alert for anything that adds to my knowledge in that area.

Sometimes it comes from quite unlikely sources.
Recently I was having trouble sleeping.
As usual my thoughts ranged far and wide.
I thought my wife's friend asking me the value of an artist's paintings.
The artist has been a professional artist for the whole of a long adult life.
How many paintings has he produced over the years?
Certainly a lot I imagine.

I thought about whether anyone had produced prints of the paintings.
I thought that was possible but I did not know.
How much might he have earned if he'd sold copyright to **ALL** works.
Not just those used for prints.
At $1 it would be as much as the works sold over his painting life so far.
Anyone who bought a painting would pay a $1 for the copyright.
Then I thought that $10 would even have attracted just as many sales.
If he has sold 5000 paintings then that is $50,000 he could have earned.
What if copyright was sold for $100?

If small cheap works they may not be interested but some would.
Many of those who owned bigger and more expensive works might buy.
That could be $100x2000 or $200,000 extra he could have earned.
This is not new thinking for me but linking it to a possible career output was.
Then I thought if he wanted to he could still earn that $200,000.
IF he has the names and addresses of the buyers - again not a new thought.
Do you collect the names and contact addresses of all who buy your work?

There are many spin-offs from this that I will not develop further here.
The idea underscores a need for professional artists to have a contact list.

It's never too early or too late to start.
It is essential in order to open up income earning avenues with past clients.

I asked some artists who are in their 80's several questions.
Here is what I found out I didn't need exact numbers, a best guess was fine.

A full time professional artist did about 3000 works and most were sold.
The average value of a typical work **NOW** is $15,000.
Only one or two works were sold as prints.
The lifetime value of works by this artist at recent prices is $45,000,000.
The copyright (at 10% of present value) is worth $4,500,000.
More if major works are the focus.
The artist finds 10% who buy copyright there is at least $450,000 for asking.
That's as good as winning the lottery!

Over a career another full time professional did about 3000 works too.
Again most were sold at an average value.
An average work **NOW** is $1,200.

The artist sold copyright for many works with substantial print income.
But even then only about 200 works have had their copyright sold.
Lifetime value of works produced by this artist at recent prices is $3,600,000.
The copyright value (at 10%) is $360,000.
If the artist finds 10% of them to buy copyright there's $36,000 just for asking.
Still a handy sum for an elderly artist as I'm sure you will agree.

Copyright can provide at least some of your retirement income.
The artists mentioned above illustrate the potential contribution.
Provided you have been collecting contact details during your active years.
If not then it's never too late to start!

I have only written about selling copyright.

You can sell copyright **and** gain referrals.

Will those who own works displayed in prominent places be interested?

Often it is part of a business image and copyright lets them capitalize on that.

Do you sell copyright?

Why not?

Chapter Five: Business details.

    1. Always have a plan in business dealings.

    2. Add-ons

    3. Selling copyright to your art through a gallery.

1. Always have a plan in business dealings.

Buying or producing something for sale things you should know.
What you can sell for, who a client is or likely to be, and conditions of sale.
The information is there so create a proposal with a good chance of success.
Let's look at those aspects a little more in relation to selling copyright.

What can you sell copyright for?
Past history is the guide here.
That's where a publisher has a considerable advantage over most artists.
The publisher knows from previous experience what copyright is worth.
Most artists have no idea.

What prices have you actually obtained in the past?
Have your copyrighted reproductions sold easily or have sales been a while?
Has the publisher (or you) experimented with price, upwards, and down too?
In other words do you have adequate information to set a reasonable price?
If not, then consider market research to establish a suitable starting point.

You are considering selling copyright to your clients.
They have bought or are considering buying one of your works.
My advice is always start low so that at least a sales pattern is commenced.

Possibly a 10% premium for copyright is a good place to start.
That can be justified as equivalent the amount an author earns for copyright.
Perhaps even 5% could be a start?
The important thing is to actually start selling copyright and make sales.

Establish a sales history then it's possible to consider.
Maybe 5% could become 10% in certain circumstances.
A condition might be all work under a particular price range (less than $500).
If sales continue at the higher level, then that could be the standard price.
You can continue adjusting the copyright premium until you reach a barrier.
When that happens back off a bit and stabilize at that price level.

What does the barrier relate to?
Is it certain prices for the works (high or inexpensive)?
Perhaps for certain subjects, different sizes, in geographic areas, or what?
Keep experimenting while you do not have answers.
A copyright premium low at a new venue and high where you're established?
The knowledge gained from experimentation applies to original works too.

Who is your client?
You may know the names of actual clients, and that's a good thing.

People who bought copyright of a work once are likely to buy again.
Knowing who they are you can target them in your copyright marketing.
Some own multiple works, so are potential buyers of copyright for each one.
They never know when they might want to reproduce one of your paintings.
So they should really buy copyright for all of them, shouldn't they?

In addition work out something about the kind of people they are.
Can you guess at their incomes?
What sorts of jobs do they hold?
Are they married or single?
What age bracket do they fall into?
Knowing this information means you can then identify other similar people.
They are reasonable prospects for sales of your works and thus copyright.

What conditions of sale are feasible and will you accept offers?
What will you say to such a request?
Work out what is reasonable and be prepared for what a client may propose.
How does selling copyright fit into this scenario?

When selling their works, many artists are not prepared to negotiate.
Often this is because someone else is doing the selling on their behalf.
They aren't willing to, or haven't the authority to, negotiate.
They negotiate buying a car, electrical goods, furniture or a house.
Why the different attitude?

It's cultural. In everyday affairs it's fairly normal to negotiate a price.
Except auction, no-one expects to pay asking price if house selling or buying.
We set fixed prices on works and resent potential clients who negotiate.

Why should someone obtain a reduction just because they ask?
Actually they shouldn't for you should get something in return for a reduction.
It is possible to increase value without reducing price.
You can even gain value with a reduced price by using add ons.

That's really the crux of the discussion, gaining value.
Negotiating is about both buyer and seller gaining value.
Negotiating happens when someone has something the other person wants.
Both are prepared to bargain for it.
It doesn't just happen when buying and selling.
Negotiating is about resolving an issue between two people, or groups.

Perhaps first consider whether you should negotiate or not?
Do you feel comfortable negotiating?
This might be negotiating generally or on this particular occasion.
It's up to you, if you don't want to, there is no negotiation.
Then the other person has to buy on your terms or they don't buy!
Many sales take place on this basis.
If you're uncomfortable you'll not be happy with an outcome from negotiation.

Will you get what you want from the discussion?
That's important, because if you don't get it then you've lost.
You probably would have been better not negotiating at all.
Weigh up if is it better to sell at a lower than desired price, or not sell at all?

Only you can decide.
In those markets where bargaining is normal behaviour.
The seller usually starts with a higher price than they expect to obtain.

Is there room for reduction and still get what you want, or better?
Does your price contains a margin for negotiating?
You are more likely to obtain a satisfactory price outcome from that process.
Should you do that?
Could your copyright premium be that margin?

Plan your negotiation.
Let's say you're interested in negotiating the sale of one of your works.
Just how should you go about it?
If you are prepared you have a better chance of a satisfactory outcome.

Develop your own negotiating strategy.
Which means you'll be prepared for any situation where negotiating is likely.
Selling copyright is no different, except it may be a lever to sell the work.
Many politicians have reputations as negotiators.
There are many other people who are also considered good negotiators.
They aren't people who have strong views on the negotiation outcomes.
They just want to see an outcome.

Obviously the quality of a database is the key to many residual sales.
If you can't contact people then you can't sell them anything at all.

What data is important and what isn't?
Will currently unimportant information be important in one year?
Three years or five?
What haven't you thought of?

2. Add-ons

Selling copyright is a powerful added value that brings extra sales.
As well as extra income from each sale.
It really costs nothing to try.
Perhaps you are not sure what I'm getting at?

You (or gallery) could advertise your works for sale at the normal price.
Then for no extra or another 10% (you choose) the client can have copyright.
They can print their own cards without any hassle (etc.).
This says buying a work doesn't automatically mean the copyright is bought.

In business, the best way to attract clients is to provide better value.
This may mean better value than the opposition, or better value than normal.
Obvious ways to do this are by a cheaper price or, a better quality product.
Or even a better quality product for the same price.
Another way is provide an extra service or product at no, or little, extra cost.

When this is done a business gives better value providing an 'add-on'.
For example, buy one widget and get another free.
They are basically bonuses people receive with a purchase.
You will have seen buy a Big Mac and get French Fries for half price.
Once you start to look 'add-ons' are everywhere.

They're everywhere because quite simply they work.
You may see promotions if you buy a limited edition book get an etching too.
Maybe that should really be, buy an etching and get a free book?
No matter, either way it's an example of an 'add-on' to provide better value.
It's a more attractive package than either element by itself.

'Add-ons' are a different kettle of fish from discounts.
In order to take advantage of the offer, the client has to buy at the full price.
You get your money back for the 'add-on', or it actually costs very little.
You still make the full amount on the sale itself.
With a discount you reduce your profit in the hope of extra sales.

An 'add-on' is still profitable whatever the volume of sales.
The 'add-on' can stimulate extra sales, over and above normal expectations.
It all depends on how it is done.

It's possible to use the 'add-on' technique as a standard sales method.
But there's a danger it will lose effectiveness over time.
Eventually the two elements of an 'add-on' become the normal unit.
This may be good value compared with others, but it won't be for you.

Attract new clients but 'add-ons' are decreasingly effective for regulars.
This isn't necessarily bad, but it could be better.
Particularly because regular clients are probably the best.
So, it's much more likely you'll use 'add-ons' for special situations.
In the real world this is what happens too.

You can't get half price French Fries all the time, only at special times.
The 'add-on' is used by McDonalds to get extra clients when they want them.
It's not likely to be during school holidays, is it?
Like McDonalds 'add-ons' can help with specific sales or marketing problem.

Getting people to buy at over $1000 for the first time is difficult.
This is particularly so, if you are new to the client.
Perhaps your work is at a gallery where you have never previously exhibited.
Give an incentive, or 'add-on', so potential or past clients break the barrier?
If you can, it might be worth a try, mightn't it?

How about providing copyright free in those circumstances?
It doesn't cost you any actual money and adds value for the prospect.
The copyright is still given a value (say $100).

Over time you adjust the threshold above which someone must spend.
Before they receive free copyright.
As you are more popular and sell at higher prices the barrier can be raised.
Possibly there could be an additional 'add-on' bonus.
Maybe the 'add-on' can be eliminated, as it may no longer be necessary.

Like McDonalds and other businesses, always conditions apply.
Before people get an 'add-on' they must buy a 'Big Mac', or spend $1000.
It's not usually sufficient that people just buy.
In your case, they must be certain kinds of people (haven't bought before).
They might be buying at a particular price level.
Or a certain kind of work, at a particular time, in a certain place, and so forth.

There are lots of situations where you can use copyright as an 'add-on'.
Each one could help you add to your bottom-line.
If you think along these lines you can invent your own add-on promotions.

3. Selling copyright to your art through a gallery.

A gallery does not exist so any artist has a place to show his/her work.
A gallery shows work by a poor struggling artist if they think sales are there.
Either now or possibly in the medium term.
A gallery exhibits work by artists because it is a proven effective way to sell.
So let there be no mistake, your relationship with a gallery is a business one.
The objective the exchange of money that follows a sale.
Selling copyright through a gallery is just part of this arrangement.

There are three ways a business that sells, can acquire stock.
Manufacture it themselves.
Purchase it from a manufacturer.
Hold the work on consignment, paying the manufacturer after the sale.

You are the manufacturer of your artworks.
It thus follows that you can sell them yourself.
This could be at a retail level direct to the client (from your studio or gallery).
You can sell on a wholesale basis to someone who in turn retails it.
Selling copyright follows similar principles.

The wholesale price must be less than the retail price.
Otherwise a retailer can't make money!
They have to sell at a higher price than others (you).
The retailer is has the risk (large in the case of artwork) the work will not sell.
It is usual in slow moving retail areas for markups to be high to compensate.
Quick selling lines (like food) may only have a markup of a few percent.
Jewellery can be 150% or even more.
Selling copyright is similar as both wholesaler and retailer must make money.

If you wish to sell direct to a gallery.
Your price must be such they can make money when they sell to the client.

As mentioned above you may also have your work on consignment.
Then you are paid after a sale.

This approach eliminates the risk factor for the gallery.
That means you bear the risk of the work not selling.
But the gallery still has the cost of selling.
Selling copyright follows similar principles.

Due to the slow moving nature of art sales (more works than buyers).
Consignment selling is quite common.
It is in real estate too for the same reasons.

But even here the retail seller still has to make money.
Otherwise they go out of business!
The amount earned from a sale on consignment is called a commission.
There is **NO** commission earned unless there is a sale.
Similarly there is no copyright sale unless there is a retail or wholesale sale.

If you wish to sell to a gallery, prices must be so they make money.
When they sell to a client the amount made compensates for works not sold.
Adding copyright to the sales bundle does not change these facts.
It does make selling easier as the seller has a bargaining chip to use.
They can sell the work and copyright, no copyright, or with free copyright.
In each case the work is sold at the regular price.

Let's clarify this with an example.
Joe Bloggs (an artist) sells from his studio gallery.
The price for each work varies but let's call it $A for artist's price.
Sold on consignment a wholesale price to the artist is:
$A – c (commission).
If a gallery, dealer or someone else **buys** to resell the wholesale price is:
$A –c – rf (risk factor).

Joe has a work which he sells for $1000.
The payment Joe receives when sold on consignment is $600.
(40% commission).
It's not easy but direct to a wholesaler he might receive $300 or $400.
Or what he can negotiate.

These sorts of figures are the reality of the business world

But Joe could allow the gallery or dealer to also sell the copyright.

What is the least you accept for a work in each of the three situations?

This means you know what the score is and can plan accordingly.

Then you can make decisions about the copyright premium as well.

Chapter Six: Wrapping up.

1. A good idea is for permission to be in writing.
2. Is there a standard form for copyright?
3. Here is a sample of a copyright certificate.
4. Resale price maintenance is NOT about copyright.

1. A good idea is for permission to be in writing.

There's documentation with what exactly is covered by an agreement.
There is also less likely to be a dispute about what was covered.
So, what should be covered in a copyright agreement?

Document with permission to own copyright should cover these points.
Who is giving permission (you) and who is receiving it?
State you are the owner of copyright.
NOT granted rights to this work to others inconsistent with the agreement.

Offer compensation if this information is later found to be incorrect.
It costs you nothing, but provides some protection for the copyright buyer.
Assignment of rights to the new owner of copyright, or an exclusive license.
This entitles the new owner to sue for infringement by someone else.
Must be in writing to be legally valid.

Describe the work(s) to which copyright is being assigned.
You could supply a copy of the work (photograph) as part of this description.

Set out clearly what you give permission for the copyright buyer to do.
You can assign or license just some of the copyright rights.
It's also possible for you to retain some specified rights and sell all else.
You may give exclusive non-exclusive licenses but set out what is the case.

How long does the permission to copy last?
It may be for the full period of copyright or something less (a sunset clause).

What territory is covered?
This could be local, in Australia or wherever you decide and they agree on.

What do you get?
Set out payment and/or other benefit that you get from this arrangement.
It goes without saying it's a good idea if you receive a benefit from this sale.
Money is the best benefit, but there are other possibilities.
You should also say when you are to receive this.
On signing the document is best.

Set out your requirements for attribution, and in regard to alterations.
You could also state what they should do to prevent unauthorized copying.
This may be difficult to prevent when images are digitized.

Finally sign and date the agreement.
Both you and the other party need to do this.

Perhaps your country is a party to international copyright treaties?
You'll be protected in countries which are also parties to those agreements.
You'll need to check in your own country to ascertain if there are differences.

2. There is no standard form for copyright!

There is no standard form, but it's obvious there could be.
Artists have standard forms to show authenticity of their works, mainly prints.
A similar form could be developed to cover the sale of copyright.

There should be something in writing in cases of ownership disputes.
Misunderstanding can occur at a later date.
The buyer actually needs evidence to show they've bought the copyright.

Mere possession of the work does not show ownership of copyright.
Actually possession might not even show legal ownership of the work!

A receipt is needed to show ownership.
Thus a receipt, endorsed to show ownership of copyright, is the least you do.

You could develop a 'copyright ownership' certificate.
Start by taking the 'certificate of authenticity' idea, and re-working it,

This could be specially printed and look quite grand if you wanted.
On it you have the title of the work; your name (artist), medium and the size.
Include other details that will correctly help identify the particular work.
You'd need to have words such as 'the owner (whose name you will insert)
has paid for, and is entitled to, all legal copyright privileges that previously
belonged to the artist' or something similar.

Perhaps you are limiting the nature of the copyright?
Then that will need to be stated.
Along the lines of 'except that copyright is withheld.
For the production of limited edition prints' or whatever the limitation is.
You could specify what has been bought in some circumstances. '
Copyright is limited to greeting card reproductions for owner's personal use.
But remember more limits copyright the less value it has to the purchaser.

3. Here is a sample of a copyright certificate.

Here is a sample 'Certificate of Copyright' one artist uses.
Jim Thompson (Newport, Australia) has a certificate (12cm x 8.5cm / 5" x 3").
It has the following text.

Certificate of Copyright
The owner of this painting ……………………………… (title)…………
Is granted permission to reproduce copies of this work in

……………………………………………..

(Whatever the limitations might be, if any)

………………………………………..
Signed by the artist:…………………
Signed by the client:…………………

Dated:……………..

BUT there is NO official certificate.
If you'd like something more elaborate, then that's what you should do.
Jim's certificate can provide a starting point.
Think about what you'd include on your certificate then start designing.

4. Resale Price Maintenance is NOT about copyright.

In Australia the Copyright Agency deals with Resale Price Maintenance.
Thus some readers might assume this is about copyright.

It has NOTHING to do with copyright.
It is a program where an artist can receive a share of later sales.
There are a number of conditions that need to be met.
Then the artist receives a share of the price rise above the initial one.

WHERE NEXT:

Being a professional artist is NOW harder than it ever was.
These books are on earning money from a professional art career.

Gallery Co-Operation
http://www.amazon.com/dp/B087637FFW

Selling Strategies
http://www.amazon.com/dp/B0882JH3WN

Make Exhibitions Work
http://www.amazon.com/dp/B0882MFPGX

Art Hiring
http://www.amazon.com/dp/B0884JWR2S

Agents
http://www.amazon.com/dp/B08847Y9KS

Your Website
http://www.amazon.com/dp/B08846SWQP

Courses and Workshops
http://www.amazon.com/dp/B0884B51JB

Selling Prints
http://www.amazon.com/dp/B08846SWQW

Retirement
http://www.amazon.com/dp/B0884D9TBP

Art School
http://www.amazon.com/dp/B08849FV59

TAKE THE PLUNGE and Consider a Gallery.
http://www.amazon.com/dp/B0874JF964
Hardback
http://www.amazon.com/dp/B09GQRB34T

NOT NOW:

Perhaps one of these books could interest you then?

What about your own memories?
YOU could publish them – like I did!
http://www.amazon.com/dp/B087DWKPTP

A simple way to start developing creativity.
If you are a parent, teacher or someone who meets a group regularly?
http://www.amazon.com/dp/B088T1KFQZ

The way most people start to become an artist!
http://www.amazon.com/dp/B088Y1DPL6

About some more of my memories.
http://www.amazon.com/dp/B088Y4RPL9

SEND TO:

Know anyone interested in chocolate recipes?
Send them a link then.
http://www.amazon.com/dp/B0882HK9Q9

Know anyone interested in THIS book?
COPYRIGHT - making money from copyright sales.
http://www.amazon.com/dp/B0892HWYTV